Béla Bartók

For Children

Pour les enfants
Para Niños

Piano Solo

Complete
Complet
Completo

Volume 1
Based on Hungarian Folk Tunes
D'après des airs folkloriques hongrois
Basado en Melodías Folklóricas Húngaras

Volume 2
Based on Slovakian Folk Tunes
D'après des airs folkloriques slovaques
Basado en Melodías Folklóricas Eslovacas

BOOSEY &HAWKES

AN IMAGEM COMPANY

DISTRIBUTED BY

HAL•LEONARD®
7777 W. BLUEMOUND RD. P.O. BOX 13819 MILWAUKEE, WI 53213

www.boosey.com
www.halleonard.com

Béla Bartók: For Children

Preface from the revised edition (1998), edited by Peter Bartók

Béla Bartók's series of piano pieces *For Children*, based on folk melodies, was written around the end of the first decade of the 20th century. The pieces were published shortly afterwards by the Hungarian publisher Károly Rozsnyai. That first publication was in four volumes, the first two containing a total of 42 pieces based on Hungarian folk tunes, the third and fourth containing 43 pieces based on Slovakian folk tunes.

In 1943, whilst in the United States, Bartók prepared a revised version of the collection for the publishers Boosey & Hawkes. The revisions were minimal: two Hungarian and four Slovakian songs were eliminated, there were a few minor alterations incorporating new ideas, some of the pieces previously written with accidentals had key signatures added, a few pieces were rewritten with changed meters; some fingerings were added or changed. Of the six pieces removed for this edition, four were based on folk songs whose authenticity is in doubt. Also, two Slovakian songs were in fact not set to piano by Béla Bartók, but by Mrs. Zoltán (Emma) Kodály (who translated the texts of the Slovakian songs into German for the first edition). The matter is discussed in detail by Ferenc Bónis in "The Pieces eliminated from Bartók's Piano Work 'For Children.'" [1]

The composer prepared the revised 1943 edition by using copies of the first edition on which he marked minor changes; where the changes were more extensive, fresh manuscript was written and a new version engraved. However, much of the engraving of the first edition was preserved in the 1943 edition. Publication took place in 1946, after the composer's death; it is not known if he saw final proofs prior to printing. For this new revised edition, the music has all been re-engraved.

I would like to thank Nelson Dellamaggiore for his meticulous effort in examining the sources and comparing them with the published editions.

[1] Ferenc Bónis: 'Die weggelassen Stücke aus Bartóks Klavierwerk "Für Kinder", *Wort und Musik*, Anif/Salzburg 1992.

Textual commentary

For the present corrected edition, all surviving manuscripts and other sources have been consulted:

Manuscript draft of six pieces in volume I: nos. 13, 14, 15, 16, 17, 18 (22PS1).

Manuscript of all pieces in volume I, including the two Hungarian pieces removed in 1943 (22PI-ID1).

Manuscript of all pieces in volume II, except 7, 13, 15, 16, 23-27, 31-37, 39 (22PII-ID2).

Copies of all pieces in volume II, partly in Bartók's hand and partly in that of the copyists', used for engraving the first edition (BBA 487, 499, 2015).

Manuscript prepared by Bartók in 1943 for the new engraving of the following pieces: volume I, no. 13, 14, 17, 18, 19, 26, 31, 32, 34, 35, 36; volume II, nos. 11, 16, 32, 33 (22PFC2).

Copies of the first printed edition, with modifications by the composer, used as part of the engraving copy for the 1946 edition; also a few pages of proofs for the new engraving (22PFC1).

Violin-piano transcription of some of the pieces: *Hungarian Folktunes* by Joseph Szigeti (manuscript, with some additions by Bartók).

Most of the errors found in the 1946 publication were generally of minor consequence, except the following wrong notes (references use the numbering of the pieces after the 1943 revision):

Volume I:

No. 10, bar 19, left hand: at beat 2 F (sharp) has been changed to F natural (this note was originally F, written without key signature. In the revised edition, F sharp became part of the key signature but the need for the natural was overlooked).

No. 18, bar 10, right hand: G sharp at beat 1, an engraving error, changed to G (natural).

No. 27, bar 38, left hand: G sharp at beat 1.5 changed to G natural. This note was G sharp when first written and published; the change was made by the composer in 1943. In the first printing (1946) it appeared correctly as G natural, but in a later printing reappeared as G sharp.

No. 30, bar 16, ossia: sharp added to grace note G (engraving error); bar 20, ossia: sharp added to C in the chord at beat 2 (omission in manuscript).

No. 34, bar 11, right hand: natural added to E (engraving omission in the 1946 edition; it was written as E (natural), and printed thus in the first edition; a natural was added in the 1943 engraving copy with the key signature including E flat).

Volume II:

No. 10, bar 11, left hand, third crotchet: E changed to C (engraving error).

No. 10, bar 12, right hand, fourth quaver: B changed to D (engraving error).

No. 15, bar 14, left hand: natural added to F (it was written as F (natural), and printed thus in the first edition; for the 1946 edition the key-signature of F sharp was added, but the natural sign was omitted from the engraving).

No. 24, bar 9, left hand: E changed to E flat (presumed to be an engraving error in the first edition; it was written as E (natural) and although it is possible that Bartók may have subsequently altered it, it is believed that his first written version was as he intended - compare with the note patterns in the preceding and following bars).

No. 27, bar 9, left hand: D changed to D sharp (it was written and first printed as D sharp; in 1943 the key signature was added, requiring the deletion of many accidentals - it is believed that the D sharp was accidentally removed then, although it is possible that Bartók intentionally removed it).

Other corrections concern dynamics, the exact positions and extents of crescendos and diminuendos, slurs, missing accents, tenuto/staccato marks, etc. Pedal directions have been adjusted in many places according to the manuscripts (often Bartók wanted to delay the pedal until after the first note to be held was struck). It is impractical to list the individual corrections; however, certain specific items need to be mentioned.

The corrected printed edition cannot simply be made to conform in all respects to the composer's manuscript, since he could, and sometimes did, make alterations on an engraver's proof, or for a second edition, without entering the same change in the manuscript. Engravers' proofs seldom survived, so it is not possible to tell if a change was an engraving error or the composer's change on the proof. The fact that the composer had a second chance to examine proofs, as was the case in this series of pieces, can not be construed as a guarantee that he checked every detail, other than those he marked to be changed.

Where there are discrepancies, Bartók's intended version can usually be deduced. Errors that are clearly the result of a copyist or engraver's oversight present no problem. Uncertainties can arise, however, where a certain detail was in the manuscript and in the engraving copy, but not in the printed edition; these could either be engravers' errors or composer's changes. In this edition, corrections are made in accordance with the manuscript, or as the available sources suggest would be the composer's intent. These are as follows:

Volume I:

No. 1, bars 13 and 21, right hand: the manuscript had staccatos on the fourth quavers which were missing in the first printed edition. The staccatos are added in the revised edition, as an engraver's omission is believed to be more likely than deletion by the composer.

No. 11: the direction in the manuscript and first edition was **Molto sostenuto**, without a metronome mark. In the 1943 revision this was altered to **Lento**, ♩=66. For the last seven bars of the piece, **Più sostenuto** (implying a reduced tempo) in the manuscript was left unchanged.

No. 13: this is one of the pieces for which the composer prepared a new manuscript in 1943, changing the meter from 2/4 to 4/4, increasing the note values accordingly. The left-hand accents on the second beats of bars 12 and 13 were not copied and therefore did not appear in the 1946 edition. It is believed that the accents were left off only as a copying oversight, since the principal objective of the new manuscript was the meter change; they are restored in the present edition.

No. 14, bar 12: the accent on the last crotchet was missing from the 1943 manuscript and hence omitted in the 1946 edition. However, it was present in both the original manuscript and the first edition; its omission is assumed to have been a copying oversight and so it is restored here.

No. 16: in the manuscript the grace notes in bar 5, beat 1 are demisemiquavers, but were in both instances printed with two beams. This is believed to have been an oversight on the part of the first engraver and the third beam is added to the revised edition as in the manuscript. Additionally, the slurs for the left hand are adjusted to match those in the right hand in physical dimension, even though this results in the extension of some slurs beyond the last notes affected. In the manuscript, left-hand slurs extended beyond the last note to which they applied in bars 2, 4, 6, and 10. In the first edition, the slur in bar 4 was shortened by the engraver; in the 1946 edition the slur in bar 2 became lengthened. Both slurs now follow the manuscript and match the slurs in the right hand.

No. 18, bars 8 and 9: the left-hand slur for the up-stemmed voice (from G at beat 1.5 to D in the next bar at beat 1) was not in the 1943 manuscript; it cannot be determined if it was added by Bartók or an editor, but appears to be correct.

No. 19: in the third bar before the end, a staccato mark is added to the G in the right hand at beat 4; the staccato was in the first manuscript and the first edition, but omitted in the 1943 manuscript of the piece (where the meter was changed from 2/8-4/8 to 2/4-4/4). This was probably an oversight; the staccato appears every other time in this phrase.

No. 21, bars 15 and 16: the staccato marks for the right hand down-stemmed dyads are editorial additions. They were not in the manuscript and their omission is believed to have been an oversight. In bar 18, staccatos in the left-hand part, although in the manuscript, are deleted since the direction *simile* already implies the continuation of the pattern of the preceding bar.

No. 22: the metronome mark is changed from ♩=114 to ♪=114. The manuscript and first edition had only **Allegretto**; in 1943 the metronome mark and duration of 52 seconds were added. What Bartók wrote down for tempo cannot be determined as the publishers pasted ♩=114 over his writing. Since the two are irreconcilable (the printed metronome mark would yield half the stated duration) and the melody sounds unnaturally fast at the higher tempo, the duration figure (which is in Bartók's hand) is accepted as correct and the metronome mark, believed to be erroneous, is changed.

No. 25, bar 2, right hand: the tied G is marked tenuto and staccato (like the preceding quavers) in the manuscript. Although it is unusual for such a long note to be marked staccato, it corresponds to the manuscript and so is not changed. Note, however, that in the phrase in bars 7-9 (not covered by the *simile* direction), the crotchet and minim dyads are not marked staccato; neither are the two concluding chords of the piece.

No. 29: there are many accents in the manuscript that do not appear in print: right hand, first beats in bars 19, 21, 22, 23, 24, 38, 39, and 40; left hand, first beats in bars 53 and 55. The same phrase, however, appears many times without accents in the manuscript, so the omitted accents cannot be regarded as contrary to pattern. It is assumed that they were deleted by the composer and so are not restored here. It may also be argued that the left-hand accents in bars 19, 21 and 22, playing in octaves with the right hand, should also have been removed.

No. 30, bar 4, right hand: an accent on the first D could be expected and its omission in the manuscript may have been an oversight. However, this is not necessarily the case, as the same phrase does occur without accents in the second half of the piece.

No. 38, bars 46-49: marcato accents were incorrectly printed in the first edition (in the wrong bars and for one hand only). In preparing the revised edition the composer extended the marcatos in bars 46 and 58 to both hands, probably without reference to the manuscript, and deleted those in bars 47 and 49. The present edition follows the manuscript, believed to represent his original concept.

No. 39, bars 28-35: slurs in the left hand are moved below the down-stemmed quavers as they apply to that voice.

No. 40: this piece is transcribed from a variant of the folk tune on which no. 37 (*Swine-herd's Song*) is based. It is as performed by an old peasant flautist, the last from Felsőiregh (now part of Iregszemcse), in the county of Tolna. See Bartók's cylinder recording no. 55 at the Museum of Ethnography, Budapest.

Volume II:

No. 1, bars 1 and 6: the crescendo signs are missing in previous editions; they were present in the composer's manuscript but not copied into the engraving copy. The presence of crescendos in bars 11 and 21 suggests that those in bars 1 and 6 were intended.

No. 2: previous editions have no starting dynamic; the manuscript is marked *p*, so this is added here.

No. 2, bars 5-6: in previous editions, the diminuendo is missing; it has been added according to the manuscript.

No. 2, bar 14: *pp* has been added in accordance with the manuscript; it was omitted from the first engraving copy. Its inclusion corresponds to the pattern of dynamics in the last three bars; also the *p* in bar 17 would be redundant without the preceding *pp*.

No. 7: the original Hungarian title of this song was Betyárnóta (*Song of a Vagabond*). As it is believed that Bartók approved the new title Banát (*Sorrow*), this has been retained. However, the French title remained as *Chanson du vagabond* in the first edition, from which the French titles for this edition have been taken.

No. 15, bars 6-7, left hand: ties that have been added across the barline to G and E. Although the entire chord was tied in Bartók's manuscript, only the C was tied in the copyist's copy; this omission had not previously been noticed.

No. 18, bar 23, left hand: the previously printed rhythm ♪ ♪ ♪ ♪ is corrected to ♪ ♪ ♪ ♪, in accordance with Bartók's manuscript and the copyist's copy for engraving; the error probably occurred in the first engraving and was never detected. It is possible, however, that Bartók made this change in correspondence which has not survived.

No. 24, bars 6-7, left hand: the slur was not in the manuscript, probably through an oversight.

No. 36-37, bar 106 (13 bars from the end): the first up-stemmed chord has a tenuto sign in all printed editions; this is not present in the only manuscript that can be found for this piece. It has not been deleted here as it is assumed that an engraver would be unlikely to add the tenuto mark by accident. It is more likely that it was added on the proof by the composer; it seem to anticipate the *sf* on the following chord.

No. 38, bar 42 (3 bars from the end) - bar 44: in the left hand, the unconnected tie and the lack of rests in the final bars are as in the manuscript sources, as are the unconnected ties on the final notes in the right hand. Although previous editions omitted these ties and added rests in the empty bars, there is nothing to indicate that the were removed at the composer's direction, and the fading out at the end of this piece seems appropriate.

For Children

Pour les enfants   Gyermekeknek   Para Niños

Volume 1

1. Children at Play

Les enfants en plein jeu   Játszó gyermekek   Niños Jugando

Béla Bartók
revised by the composer (1943-1945)

(32")

2. Children's Song

Chanson pour enfants   Gyermekdal   Canción para Niños

3.

* Pedal sign

down   up

4. Pillow Dance

Danse de l'oreiller   Párnatánc   Danza de la Almohada

(58")

5. Play

Jeu   Játék   Juego

(1' 5")

6. Study for the Left Hand

Etude pour la main gauche   Balkéztanulmány   Estudio para la Mano Izquierda

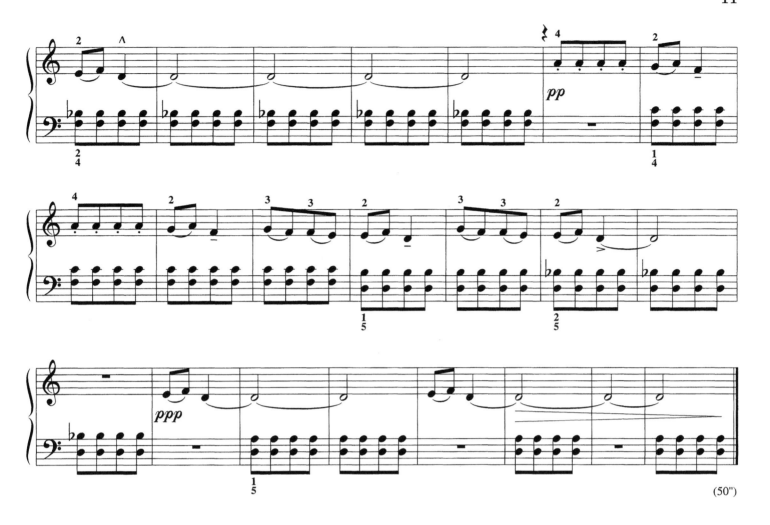

(50")

7. Play Song

Chanson à jouer   Játékdal   Canción Alegre

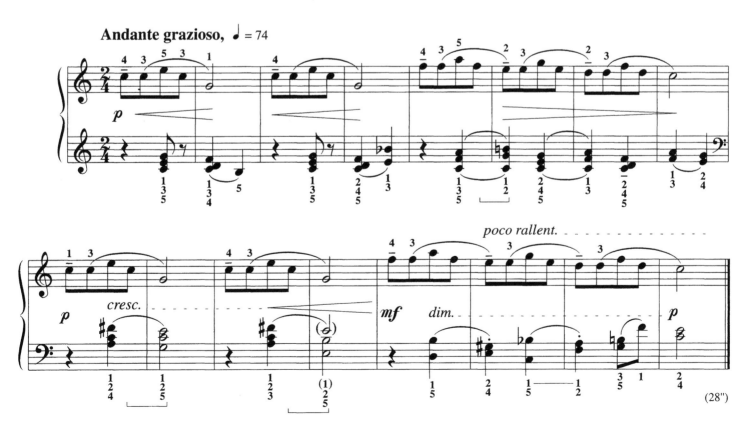

(28")

8. Children's Game

Jeu des enfants   Gyermekjáték   Juego para Niños

9. Song

Chanson   Dal   Canción

10. Children's Dance

Danse des enfants   Gyermektánc   Danza de Niños

(40")

11.

*see Textual Commentary

(56")

12.

13. Ballad

Ballade   Ballada   Balada

(1' 20")

(52")
attacca
(ad lib.)

*see Textual Commentary

14.

15.

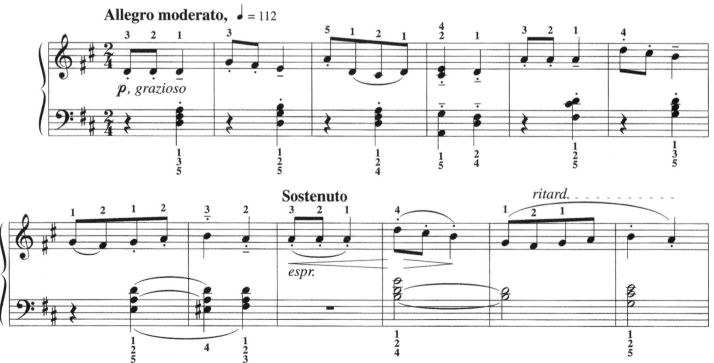

*see Textual Commentary

(28")

16. Old Hungarian Tune

Vieil air hongrois   Régi magyar dallam   Antigua Melodía Húngara

(40")

17. Round Dance

Ronde   Körtánc   Baile de Ronda

(1')

18. Soldier's Song

Chanson du soldat   Katonadal   Canción del Soldado

Andante non troppo, ♩ = 100

(1' 2")
attacca
(ad lib.)

19.

Allegretto, ♩ = 126

(40")

20. Drinking Song

Chanson à boire   Bordal   Canción Báquica

(35")
attacca
(ad lib.)

21.

Allegro robusto, ♩ = 138

(with repeat 21")

22.

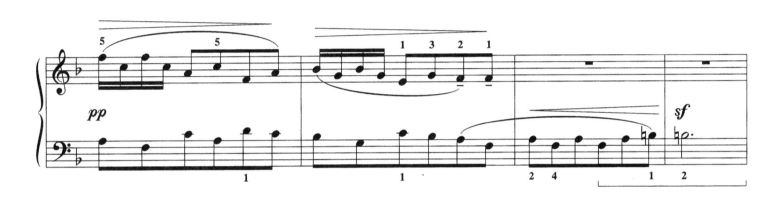

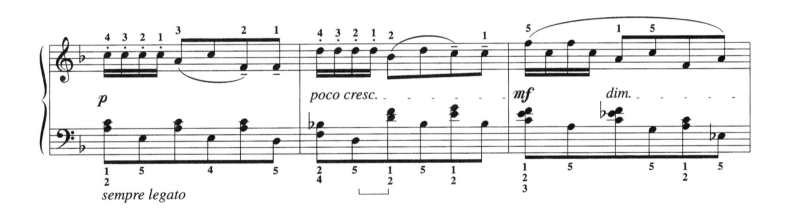

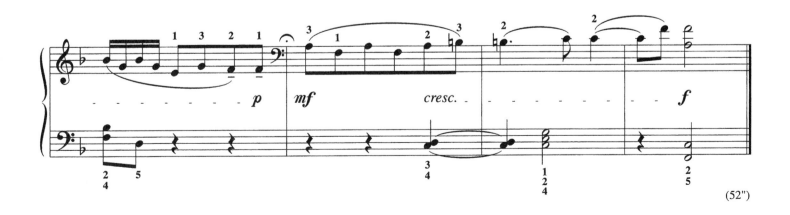

(52")

23. Dance Song

Chanson à danser   Táncdal   Canción Bailable

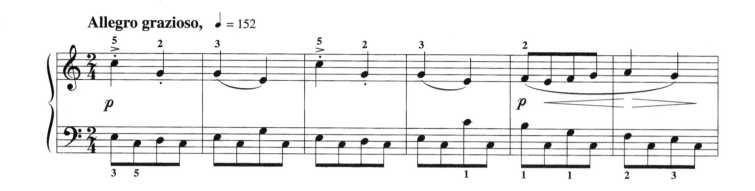

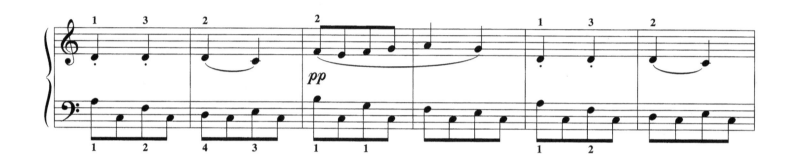

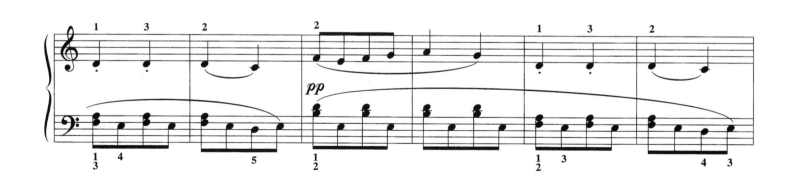

(50")

24.

(52")

25.

(37")

26.

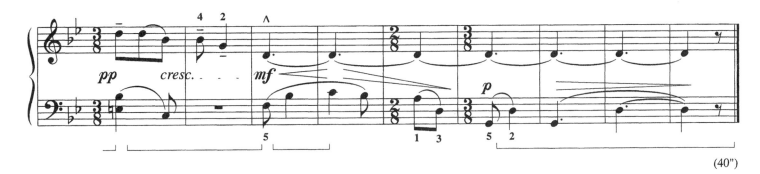

(40")

27. Jest

Moquerie   Tréfa   Broma

28. Choral

(1' 30")

29. Pentatonic Tune

Air Pentatonique   Ötfokú dallam   Melodía Pentatónica

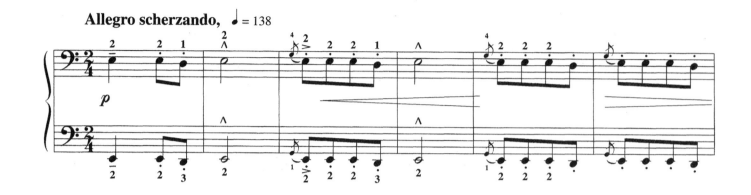

un poco marcato il tema

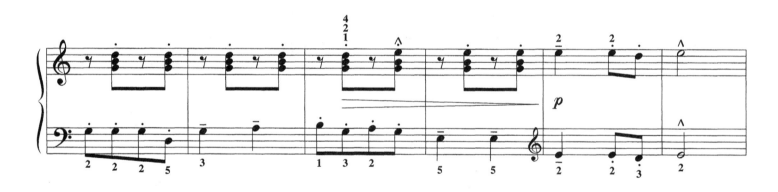

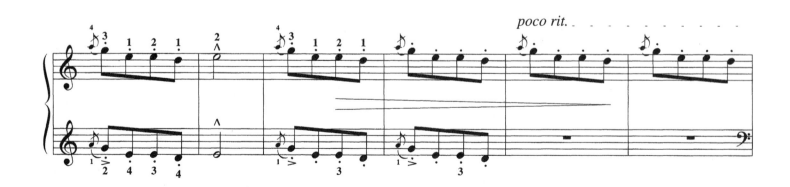

(50")

30. Jeering Song

Chanson moqueuse   Gúnydal   Canción Jocosa

Allegro ironico, ♩ = 160

(36")

31.

(1' 30")
attacca
(ad lib.)

32.

33.

Allegro non troppo, ♩ = 104

34.

35.

(27")
*attacca
(ad lib.)*

36. Drunkard's Song

Chanson de l'ivrogne   Részegek nótája   Canción Ebria

(35")

37. Swine-herd's Song

Chanson du porcher   Kanásznóta   Canción para el Porquero

(36")

38. Winter Solstice Song

Chanson du solstice d'hiver   Regös ének   Canción para el Solsticio Invernal

(1' 7")

39.

40. Swine-herd's Dance

Danse du porcher   Kanásztánc   Danza para el Porquero

(1' 45")

For Children

Pour les enfants   Gyermekeknek   Para Niños

Volume 2

1.

Béla Bartók
revised by the composer (1943-1945)

(30")
*attacca
(ad lib.)*

2.

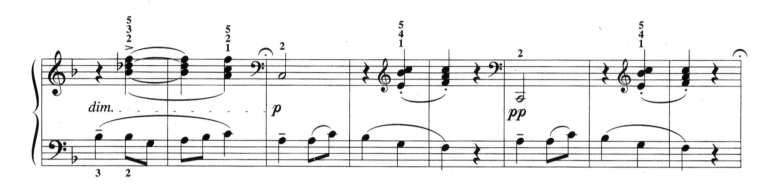

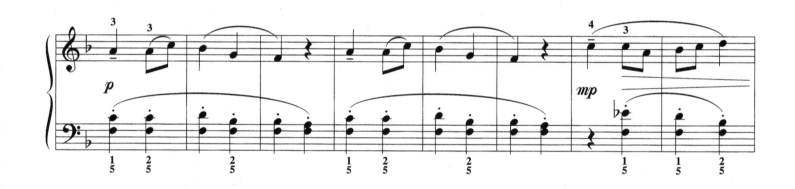

(43")
attacca
(ad lib.)

3.

4. Wedding Song

Chanson nuptiale   Lakodalmas   Canción de Bodas

(30")

5. Variations

Variations   Változatok   Variaciones

(2' 15")

6. Round Dance I

Rondo   I. Körtánc   Baile de Ronda I

Allegro, ♩ = 138

(40")

7. Sorrow

Chanson du vagabond   Bánat   Angustia

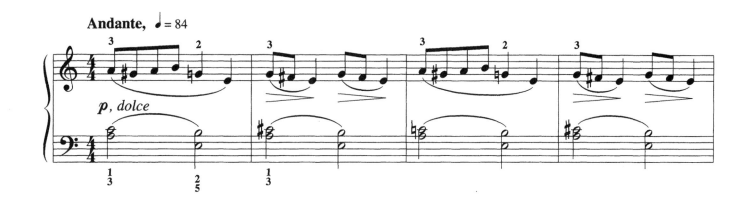

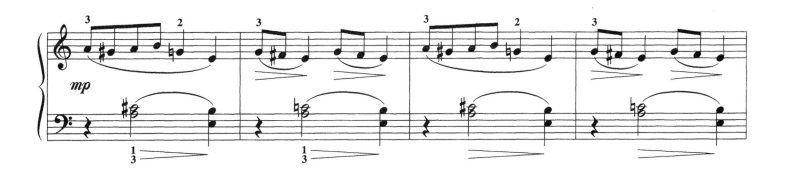

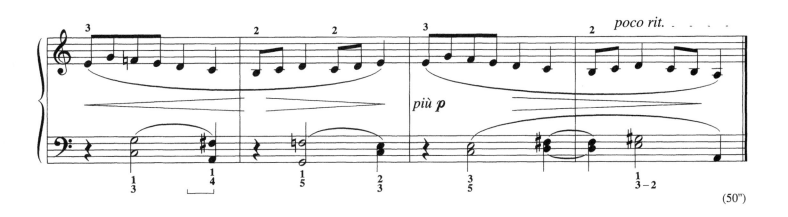

(50")

8. Dance

Danse   Táncdal   Danza

(37")

9. Round Dance II

Ronde   II. Körtánc   Baile de Ronda II

(30")

10. Funeral Song

Funerailles   Temetésre szól az ének   Canción Fúnebre

(1' 12")

11.

(1')
attacca
(ad lib.)

12.

13.

Allegro, ♩ = 132

(40")
attacca
(ad lib.)

(2x 20")

14.

(34")

15. Bagpipe I

Chanson de la cornemuse   I. Dudanóta   Gaita I

16. Lament

Plainte   Panasz   Lamento

17.

(45")

18. Teasing Song

Moquerie   Gúnydal   Canción de Burlas

(36")

19. Romance

Romance   Románc   Romance

(1' 25")

20. Game of Tag

Jeu de poursuite   Kerget dzés   Juego de Marro

(25")

21. Pleasantry

Plaisanterie   Tréfa   Humorada

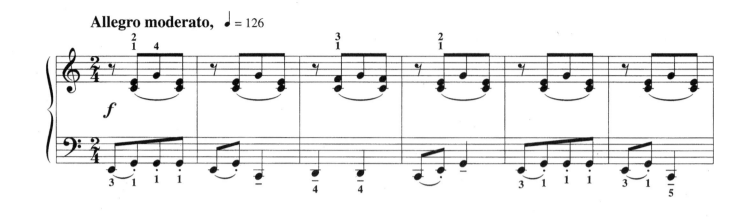

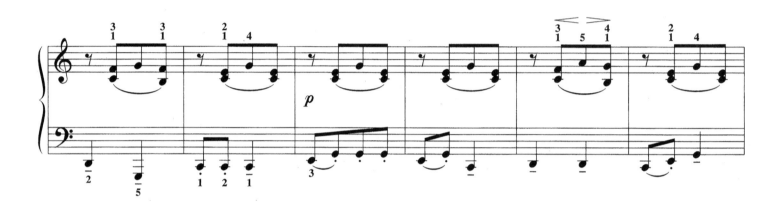

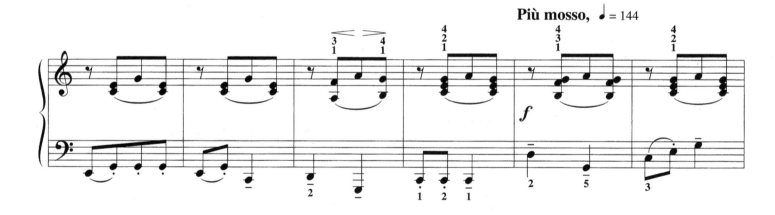

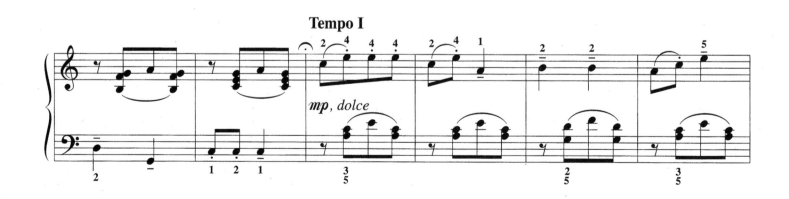

(1')

22. Revelry

Chanson de ripaille   Duhajkodó   Jarana

Molto allegro, ♩ = 152

(50")

25. Scherzando

(45")

26. Peasant's Flute

Chant fluté   Furulyaszó   Flauta campesina

27. Pleasantry II

Plaisanterie II   Még egy tréfa   Humorada II

28.

(55'')

29. Canon

Canon   Kánon   Canon

(52")

30. Bagpipe II

Cornemuse II   Szól a duda   Gaita II

31. The Highway Robber

Le "bétyar"   Betyárnóta   El Bandolero

(42")

32.

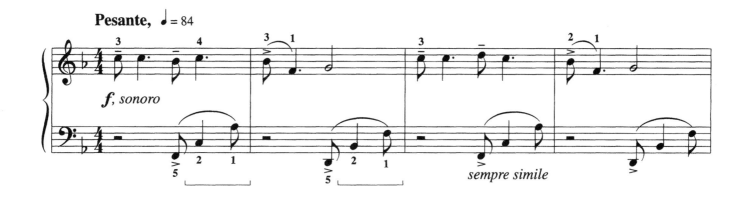

(55")

33.

Andante tranquillo, ♩ = 100

(45")

34. Farewell

Adieu   Búcsú   Despedida

35. Ballad

Ballade   Ballada   Balada

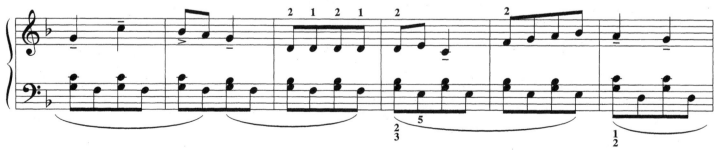

(1' 30")

36-37. Rhapsody

Rapsodie   Rapszódia   Rapsodia

(2' 5")

38. Dirge

Plainte   Siratóének   Canto Triste

39. Mourning Song

Chant funèbre   Halotti ének   Canción de Luto

Reproduced and printed by
Halstan & Co. Ltd., Amersham, Bucks., England

(2' 5")